BIRDS
COLOUR BY NUMBERS

by Sam Hutchinson
illustrated by Anna Betts

b small publishing

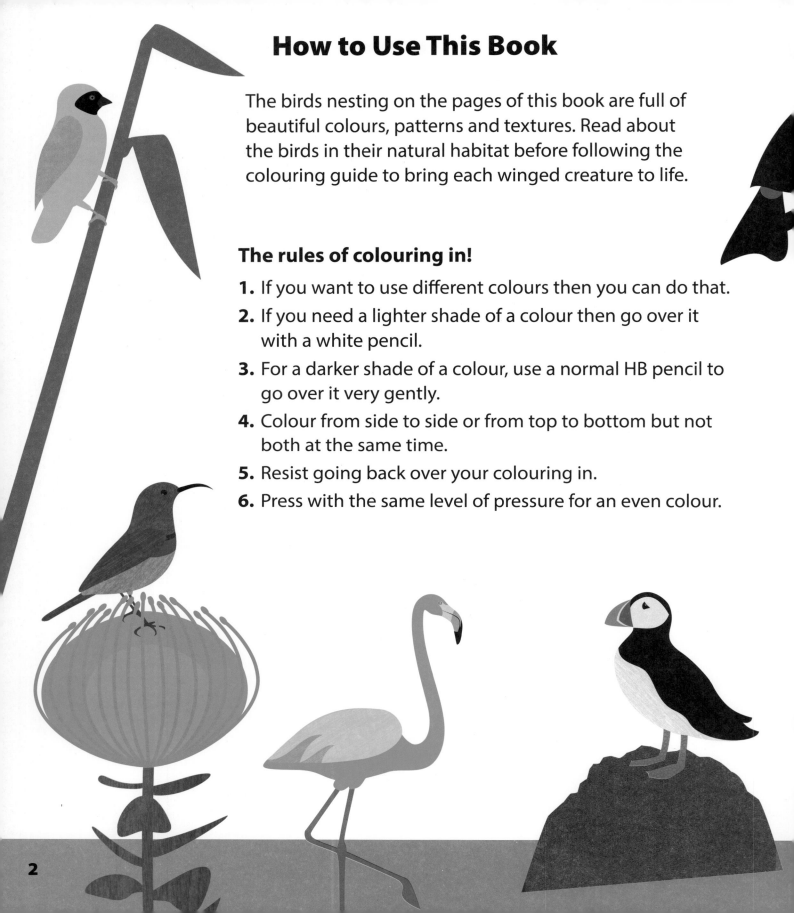

How to Use This Book

The birds nesting on the pages of this book are full of beautiful colours, patterns and textures. Read about the birds in their natural habitat before following the colouring guide to bring each winged creature to life.

The rules of colouring in!

1. If you want to use different colours then you can do that.

2. If you need a lighter shade of a colour then go over it with a white pencil.

3. For a darker shade of a colour, use a normal HB pencil to go over it very gently.

4. Colour from side to side or from top to bottom but not both at the same time.

5. Resist going back over your colouring in.

6. Press with the same level of pressure for an even colour.

Textures

Some of the patterns and textures on the birds are just for decoration. Being able to add these to your colouring in is a good skill to have.

Where the smaller shapes are darker than the background, colour in the light background first before using a darker colour to add the details on top.

If the smaller shapes are lighter than the background, draw the outlines of the lighter shapes and then colour in the dark background between them. Leave the shapes white or colour them in with a light shade.

Some textures are from a rubbing. Place some paper over a bumpy surface and colour on the paper. The pattern on the surface will show through. Wood or concrete will make a good rubbing. Copy the pattern using the above techniques or cut out the rubbing and glue it on to your drawing.

Have a bird-tastic time colouring in the birds!

4

Flamingo

Flamingos are known for their attractive pink colouring. With their feet webbed like a duck's, they can swim very well and live together in large colonies around lakes or in estuaries, where rivers meet the sea. These habitats are usually flat without many trees and very few fish so that the flamingos are not competing for food.

KEY FACTS
Size: 80 to 150 cm
Location: South America, The Caribbean, The Middle East, Africa, India and Southern Europe
Food: Algae, plants, insects, shellfish and small fish

6

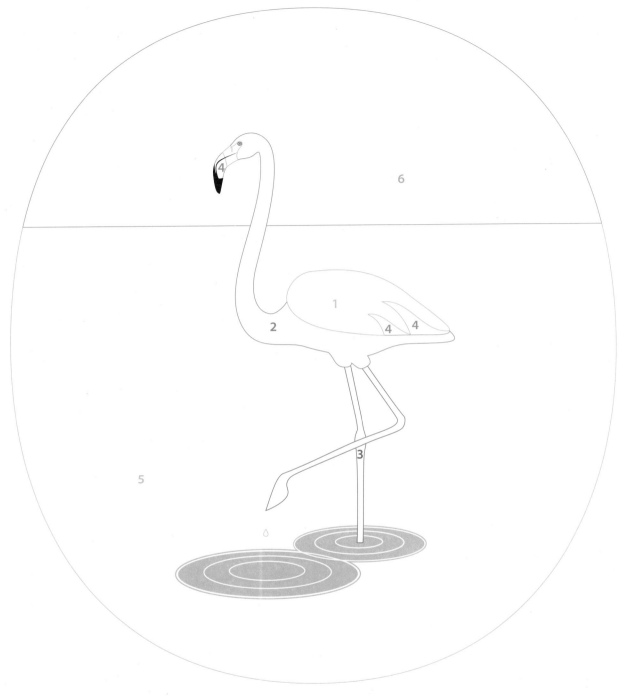

KEY

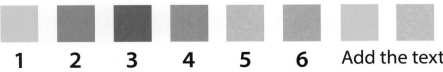

1 **2** **3** **4** **5** **6** Add the textures and patterns using the techniques from page 3.

Southern Masked Weaver

The southern masked weaver lives in lots of different types of places including woodland, grassland, wetlands and deserts. They even make their homes in people's gardens! They are called weavers because they can weave globe-style nests from reeds and grass by using complicated knots.

KEY FACTS
Size: 11 to 14.5 cm
Location: South Africa
Food: Insects, seeds, nectar

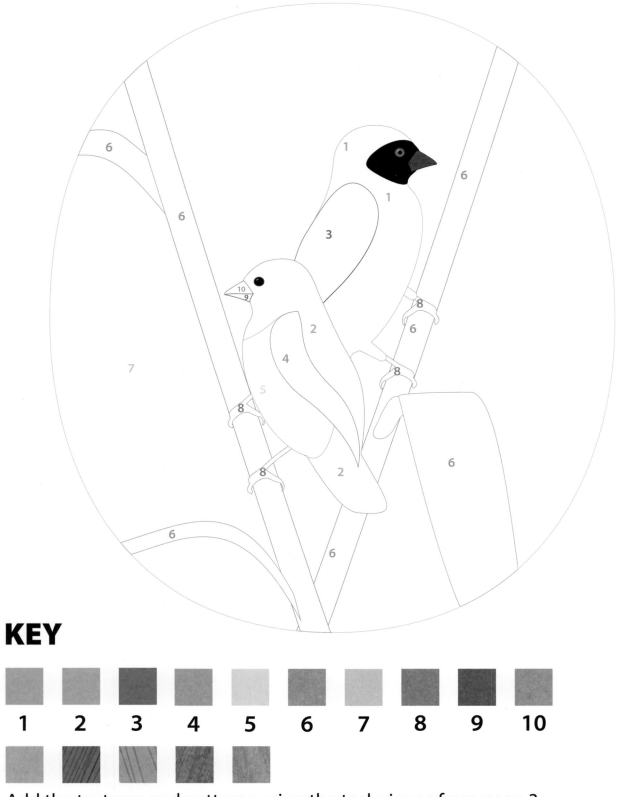

KEY

1	2	3	4	5	6	7	8	9	10

Add the textures and patterns using the techniques from page 3.

Sunbird

There are lots of small birds that have the name 'sunbird' and they are all part of the same family. Sunbirds use their long beaks to drink the nectar from flowers by perching on stalks or branches. Male sunbirds are very brightly coloured. This is so that they can attract female sunbirds.

KEY FACTS
Size: 10 to 20 cm
Location: Africa, Asia, Australia
Food: Nectar, sometimes very small insects

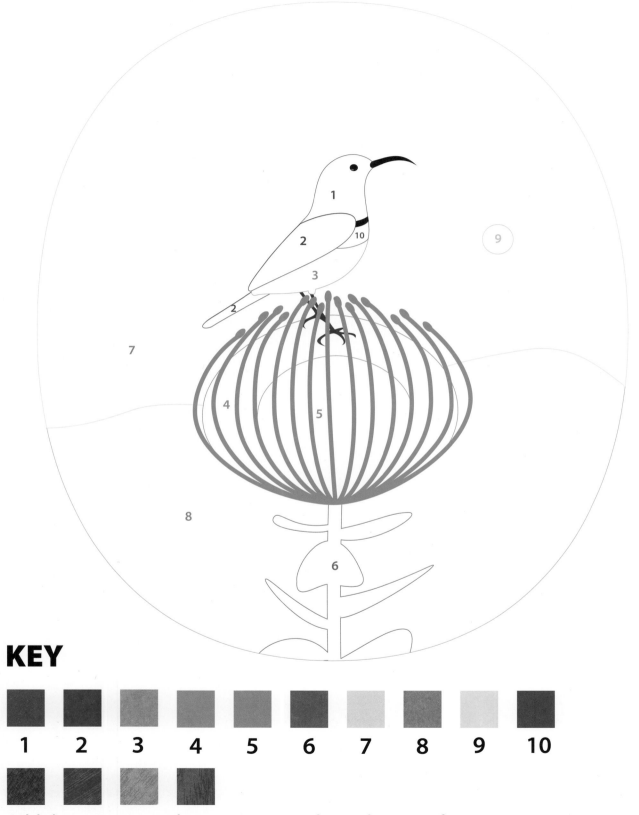

KEY

1	2	3	4	5	6	7	8	9	10

Add the textures and patterns using the techniques from page 3. **11**

Peacock

Peafowl are famous thanks to the male's spectacular tail and beautiful feathers. The male is called a peacock. Peacocks use their feathers to attract the females, which are brown in colour and called peahens. They live mostly in India but because of their beauty lots of private homes and parks around the world keep them as display animals.

12

KEY FACTS
Size: 90 to 130 cm (the tail is another 1.5 metres!)
Location: India, Java, Myanmar, Congo
Food: Insects, plants

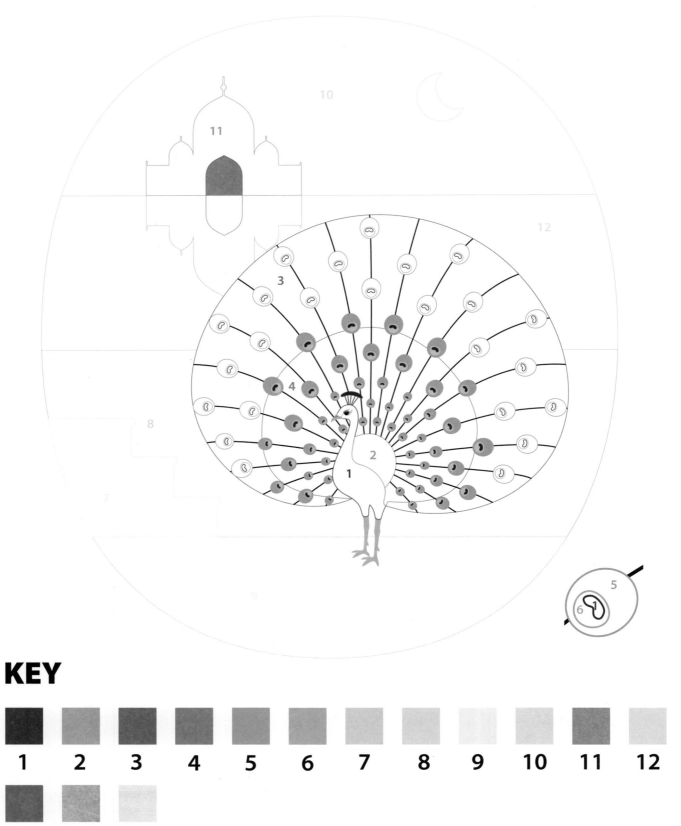

KEY

1	2	3	4	5	6	7	8	9	10	11	12

Add the textures and patterns using the techniques from page 3.

Scarlet Macaw

The scarlet macaw is the largest bird in the parrot family. They use their strong beaks to break open nuts. Easily recognisable for their brilliant red feathers and bright blue and yellow wings, these beautiful birds are in danger of losing their natural rainforest habitat. In the rainforest, these bright colours blend into the tropical surroundings.

KEY FACTS
Size: 80 cm including the tail
Location: Central America, South America
Food: Nuts, berries, fruit, insects and snails

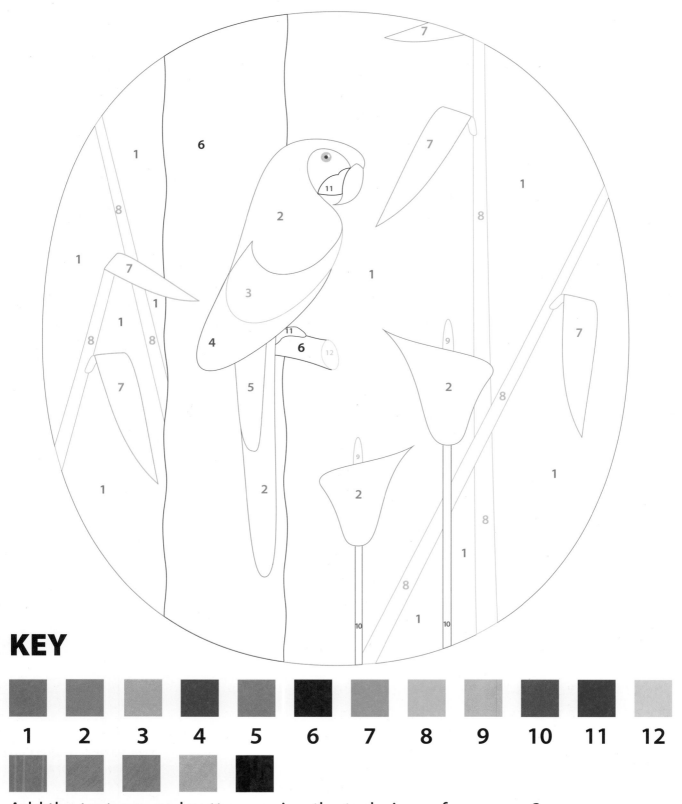

KEY

1	2	3	4	5	6	7	8	9	10	11	12

Add the textures and patterns using the techniques from page 3.

Common Kingfisher

Bright blue and orange, these small birds are incredibly fast fliers. They live near still, clear lakes or very slow-moving rivers and dive for food underwater. They swallow fish whole and then regurgitate (throw up!) the bones later in the day. In the winter, most kingfishers migrate by flying to warmer countries.

KEY FACTS
Size: 17 to 19 cm
Location: Africa, Asia, Europe
Food: Fish, aquatic insects

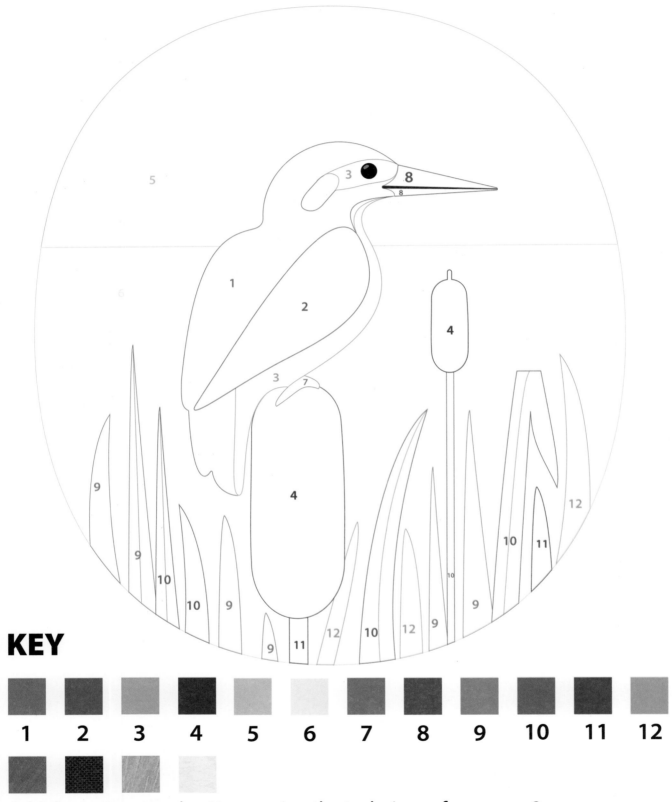

KEY

| 1 | 2 | 3 | 4 | 5 | 6 | 7 | 8 | 9 | 10 | 11 | 12 |

Add the textures and patterns using the techniques from page 3.

Hummingbird

Hummingbirds are tiny balls of energy that can fly forwards and backwards as well as being able to hover on the spot to feed. Their wings flap very quickly to create the humming sound that gives them their name. They use their long bill and tongue to reach into flowers and drink the nectar.

KEY FACTS
Size: 7 to 13 cm
Location: North America
Food: Nectar

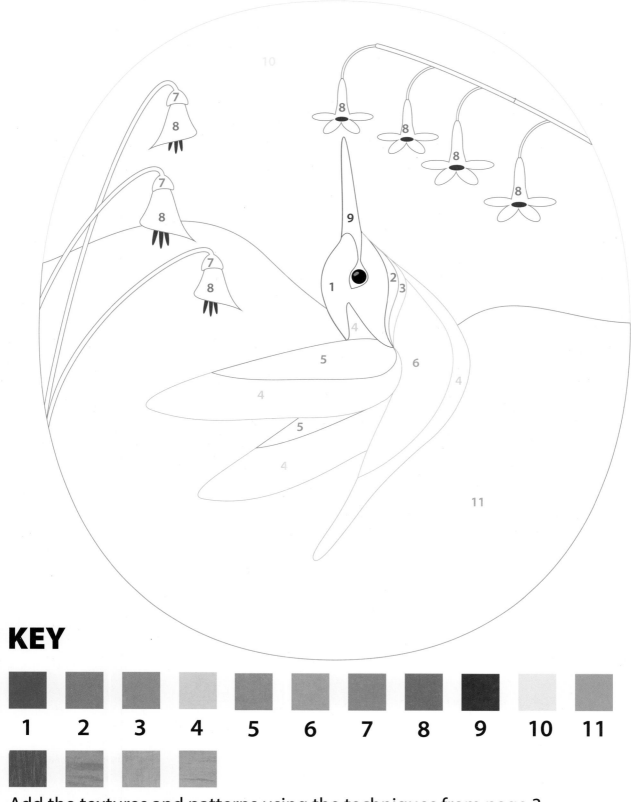

KEY

| 1 | 2 | 3 | 4 | 5 | 6 | 7 | 8 | 9 | 10 | 11 |

Add the textures and patterns using the techniques from page 3.

Toucan

In the humid weather of South America's tropical rainforests, the toucan's huge bill acts as the perfect instrument for releasing heat. The trademark bill is also used to reach fruit hanging from branches that are too thin to stand on. Because the bill is very delicate, toucans do not use it as a weapon.

KEY FACTS
Size: 30 to 60 cm
Location: South America
Food: Fruit, eggs, insects, reptiles, small animals, nuts

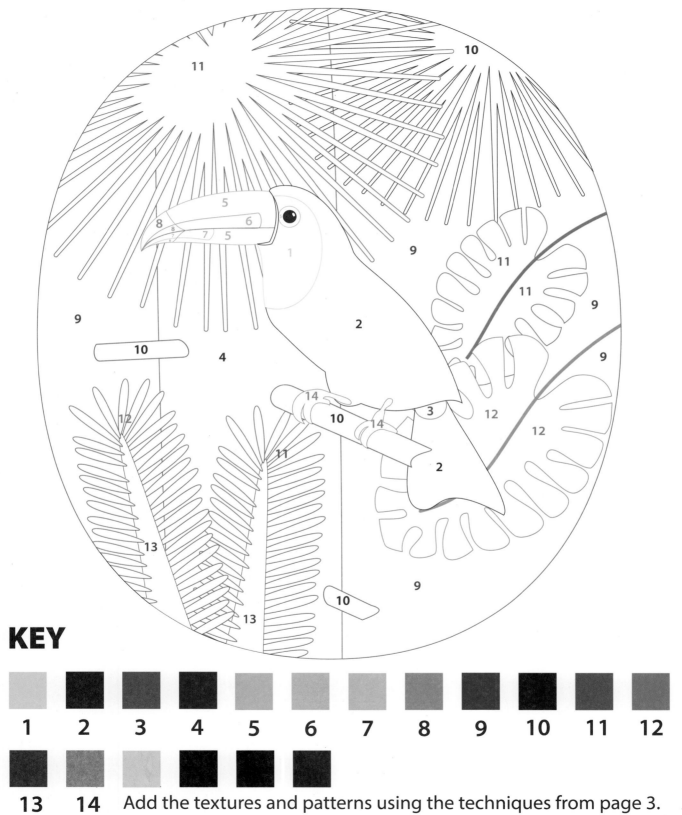

KEY

| 1 | 2 | 3 | 4 | 5 | 6 | 7 | 8 | 9 | 10 | 11 | 12 |

| 13 | 14 | Add the textures and patterns using the techniques from page 3. |

Atlantic Puffin

The puffin lives most of its life at sea, floating on the waves when it needs a rest. They hunt by diving under the surface and using their wings to fly through the water – sometimes down to 60 metres! Because of their colourful bills, some people call them the 'clown of the sea' or 'sea parrots.'

KEY FACTS
Size: 25 cm
Location: Europe, North America
Food: Fish, eels

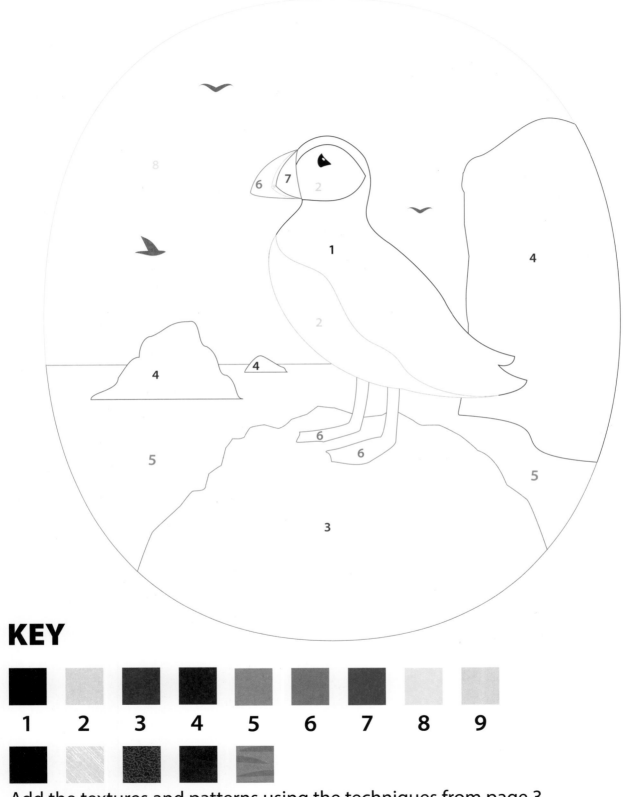

KEY

1	2	3	4	5	6	7	8	9

Add the textures and patterns using the techniques from page 3.

Golden Pheasant

Also known as the 'Chinese Pheasant', these birds can fly but not very well so they live most of their life on the ground. This is where they find most of their food. They are very good at sensing danger and can take off quickly at a very sharp angle, a bit like a big jump upwards.

KEY FACTS
Size: 60 to 100 cm
Location: China
Food: Seeds, berries, insects, plants

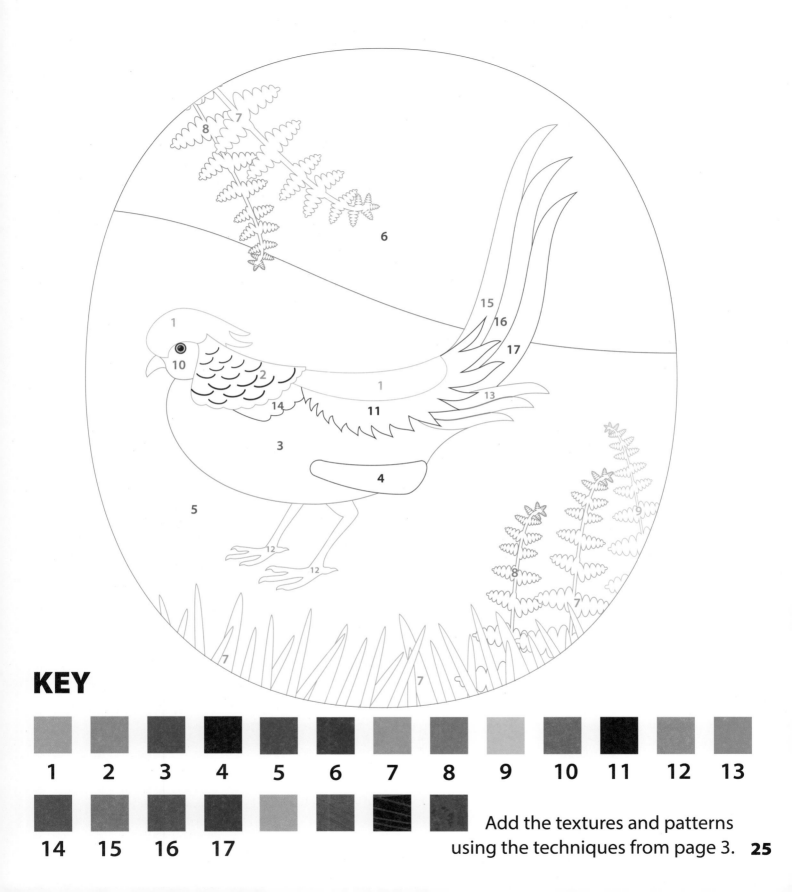

KEY

1	2	3	4	5	6	7	8	9	10	11	12	13

14	15	16	17

Add the textures and patterns
using the techniques from page 3. **25**

Woodpecker

Woodpeckers are famous for drilling into and drumming on trees. They drill nesting holes where they lay their eggs, they drill holes so that they can reach the insects underneath the bark and they also drum as a way of communicating with other birds. Two of their toes point forwards and two point backwards so that they can grip a branch as they drill.

26

KEY FACTS
Size: 14 to 58 cm
Location: Africa, Asia, Europe, North America, South America
Food: Insects, seeds, nuts

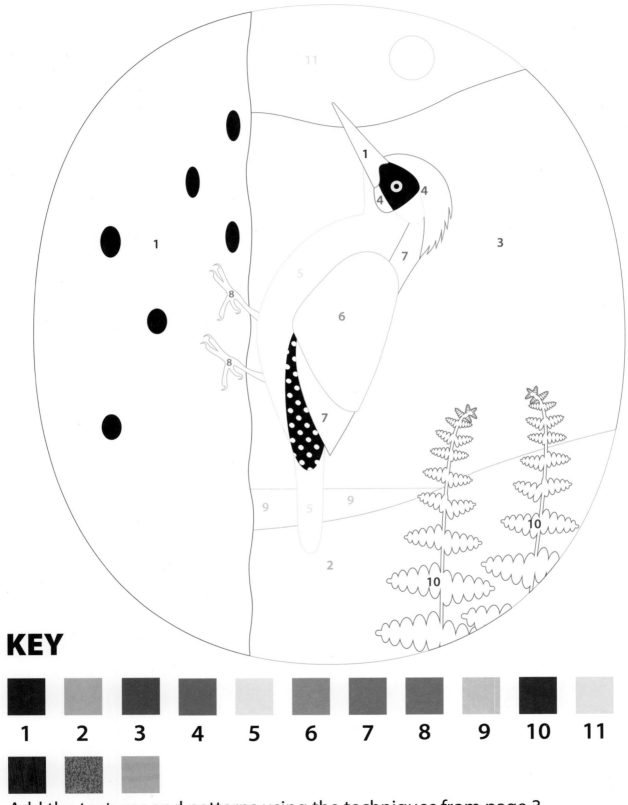

KEY

1	2	3	4	5	6	7	8	9	10	11

Add the textures and patterns using the techniques from page 3.

Mandarin Duck

This beautiful and colourful duck is originally from China and Japan. Groups of mandarin ducks now live in Europe and North America, too. They like small ponds surrounded by lots of trees and are able to fly very acrobatically through thick woods in order to reach their homes.

KEY FACTS
Size: 40 to 50 cm
Location: China, Korea, Japan, Northern Europe, North America
Food: Plants, seeds

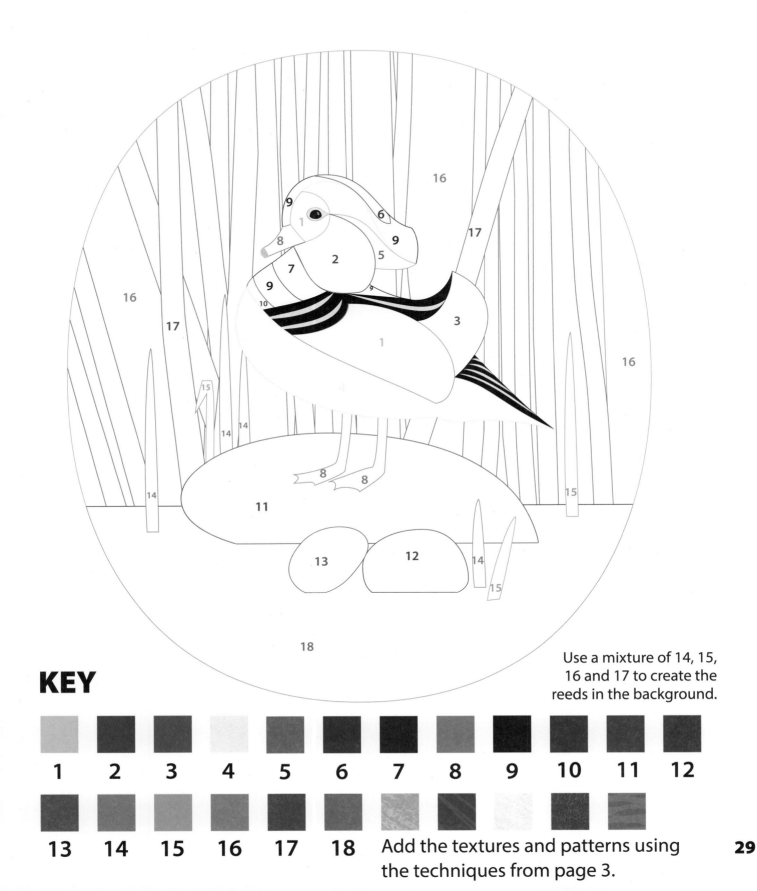

Use a mixture of 14, 15, 16 and 17 to create the reeds in the background.

KEY

1	2	3	4	5	6	7	8	9	10	11	12

13	14	15	16	17	18

Add the textures and patterns using the techniques from page 3.

Splendid Fairy-wren

Originally from Western Australia, these birds use their brightly coloured feathers to attract a mate. The male birds even bring the female birds flowers. They like to live in quiet areas away from towns, cities and people. To protect their nests from bigger birds, they cover them with grass and spiderwebs.

KEY FACTS
Size: 12 to 14 cm
Location: Australia
Food: Insects

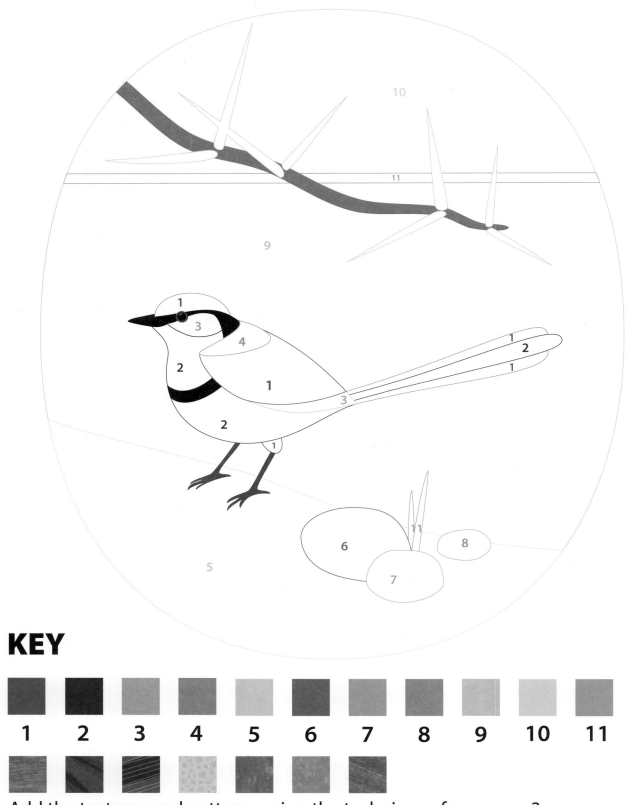

KEY

1	2	3	4	5	6	7	8	9	10	11

Add the textures and patterns using the techniques from page 3.

Draw your own birds in this tropical scene.

Published by b small publishing ltd. **www.bsmall.co.uk** Text and illustrations copyright © b small publishing ltd. 2016

1 2 3 4 5

ISBN 978-1-909767-81-2

Design: Louise Millar   Production: Madeleine Ehm   Editorial: Sam Hutchinson

Printed in China.